DO NOT REMOVE
CARDS FROM POCKET

The Deep Blue Sea

Bijou Le Tord

ORCHARD BOOKS   NEW YORK

Copyright © 1990 by Bijou Le Tord

Orchard Books
A division of Franklin Watts, Inc.
387 Park Avenue South
New York, NY 10016

Manufactured in the United States of America
Printed by General Offset Co., Inc.
Bound by Horowitz/Rae
Book design by Martha Rago
10 9 8 7 6 5 4 3 2 1
The text of this book is set in 16 point Palatino.
The illustrations are watercolor
on 100% cotton handmade watercolor paper.

Library of Congress Cataloging-in-Publication Data

Le Tord, Bijou.
  The deep blue sea / Bijou Le Tord.
    p. cm.
  Summary : Reflects on the magnificence of God's creation of the
world.
  ISBN 0-531-05853-0.—ISBN 0-531-08453-1 (lib bdg.)
  1. Creation—Juvenile literature. 2. Providence and government of
God—Juvenile literature. [1. Creation. 2. God.] I. Title.
BL226.L42   1990
231.7'65—dc20
                                                    89-16314
                                                       CIP
                                                       AC

To my editor
Karen M. Klockner

"His strength was the flowers,
his dance was the clouds."
Miguel Angel Asturias

God
made the
earth.

The sun
to warm
the days.

The moon
to cool
the nights.

And
the stars
to twinkle,
quietly.

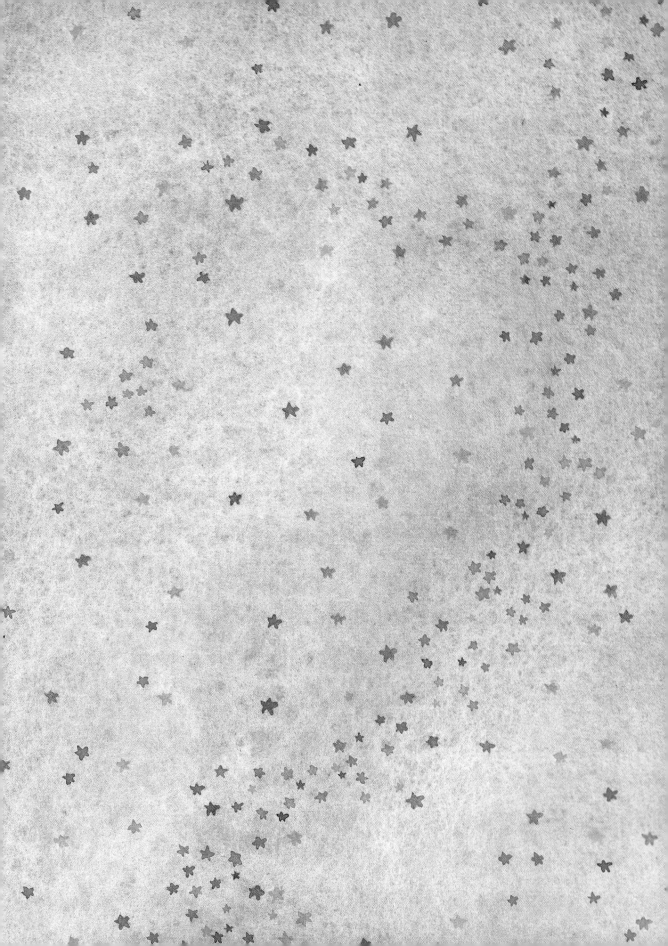

He let
drops of
rain fall
for seeds
to grow.
He planted
trees
with roots
deep in
the ground.

He planted
corn
for its yellow
grain.

He let
the streams
and rivers
flow
for birds
to nest in
cattails,
for ducks
to swim
in ponds,
and for
little frogs
to hop
on lily pads.

He made
mountains
for eternity.
Coyotes
for the desert,
snakes for
dust and
sand.

Prairie dogs
and buffaloes
for the open
plains.

He made
the wind,
the clouds,
and the deep
blue sea
for whales
to live harmoniously,

and sing
to their
sleeping
calves.

For the black-tailed gull
to swoop in
the swell of
the waves,

for the sandpiper
to feed on
tiny shrimp
and snails.

God
made volcanos,
tigers and
flowers,
bees with
honey.

He made
man and woman
to love
each other

and their children
and
their families.

He gave them
the earth
and the
planets.

He saw
that it was
all good.

God
made the
earth,
the sun,
the moon,
and the
stars
to twinkle
quietly,

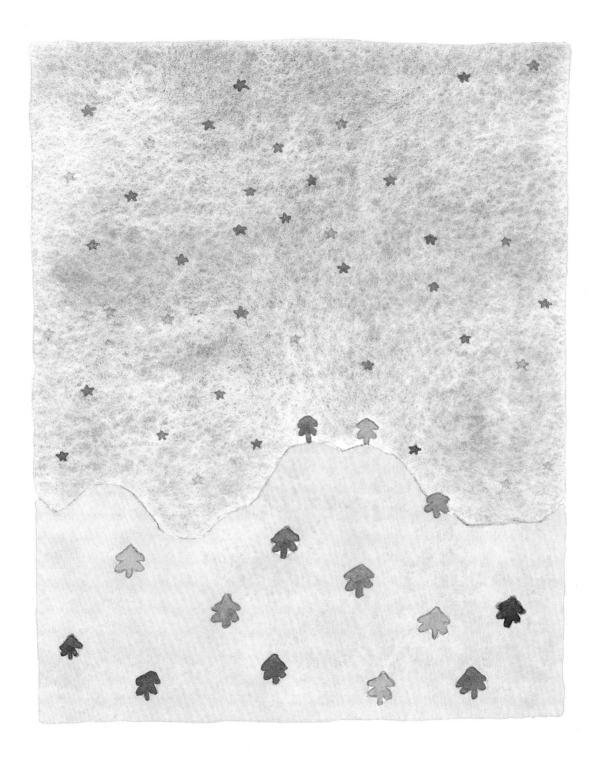

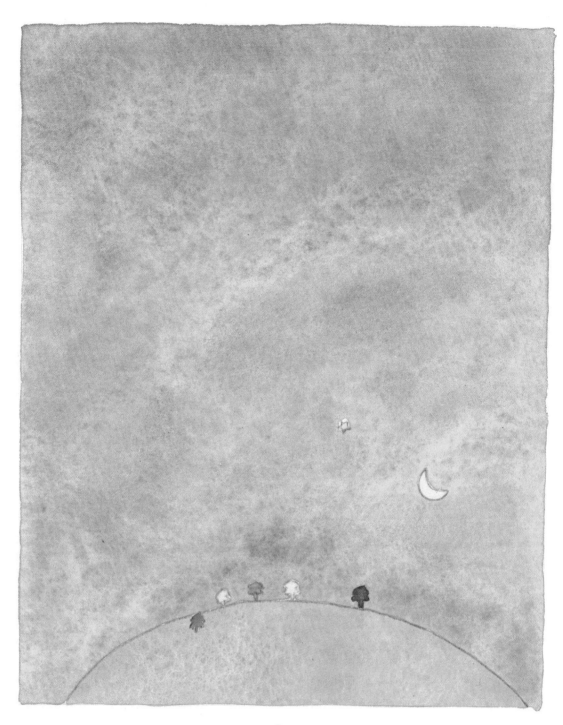

and
forever.